796.54
KLE   Klein, Adam G.
           CAMPING

DATE DUE

JA 27			
DE 2			
JE 7 -			

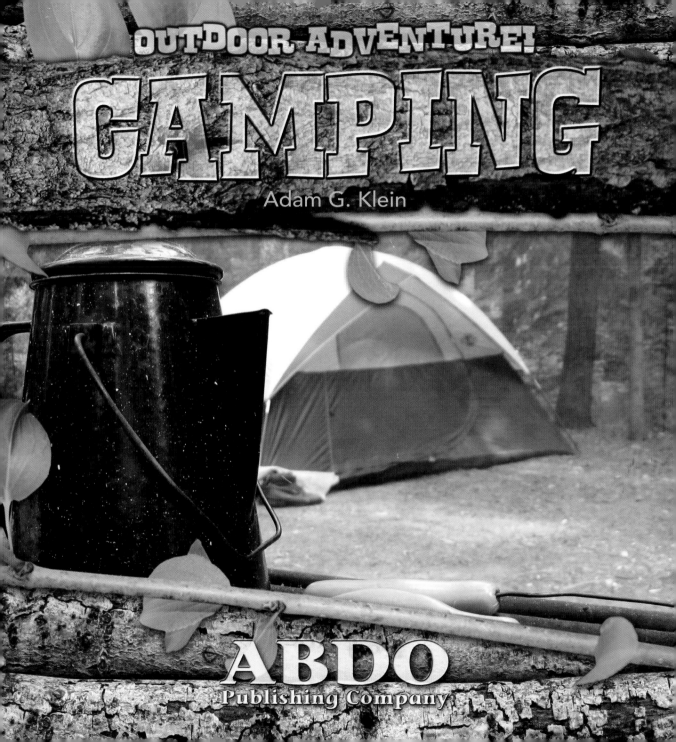

OUTDOOR ADVENTURE!
CAMPING

Adam G. Klein

ABDO
Publishing Company

visit us at
www.abdopublishing.com

Published by ABDO Publishing Company, 8000 West 78th Street, Edina, Minnesota 55439.
Copyright © 2008 by Abdo Consulting Group, Inc. International copyrights reserved in all
countries. No part of this book may be reproduced in any form without written permission from the
publisher. The Checkerboard Library™ is a trademark and logo of ABDO Publishing Company.

Printed in the United States.

Cover Photo: iStockphoto
Interior Photos: Alamy pp. 5, 21, 25, 27; Corbis pp. 7, 13, 28; Getty Images pp. 15, 17, 19, 20;
    Index Stock p. 9; iStockphoto pp. 1, 6, 16, 22, 24; Neil Klinepier pp. 11, 23;
    Photo Researchers, Inc. p. 10

Series Coordinator: Rochelle Baltzer
Editors: Rochelle Baltzer, BreAnn Rumsch
Art Direction & Cover Design: Neil Klinepier

Library of Congress Cataloging-in-Publication Data

Klein, Adam G., 1976-
 Camping / Adam G. Klein.
     p. cm. -- (Outdoor adventure!)
 Includes index.
 ISBN 978-1-59928-957-1
 1. Camping--Juvenile literature. I. Title.

 GV191.7.K54 2008
 796.54--dc22
                                    2007029165

CONTENTS

DEER AT DAWN

Joe was snoring loudly when he felt a tap on his shoulder. "Wake up, Joe," said his grandpa. But Joe was too tired to even open his eyes. Playing at the lake all day had worn him out. He rolled over and tried to go back to sleep. "Joe, you have to see this!" his grandpa persisted.

Groggily, Joe rubbed his eyes and sat up in his sleeping bag. He peered out into the campsite. The damp air was clouded by early morning fog. Squinting, Joe saw something move near the trees. What was it? Joe's eyes widened. "No way, cool!" he whispered.

A group of deer had wandered into the campground from the forest. They stayed near each other and nervously looked around as they crossed through the trees. Yet, their large eyes and rigid **stance** made them appear more noble than fearful. Silently, Joe and his grandpa watched the deer walk on.

Your best chances to see deer are in the early morning and in the late afternoon. At these times, they feed on grass or twigs. They usually rest at midday and at night.

WHY CAMP?

Camping is a great way to spend a family vacation. It allows people to discover new places and experience nature. Many adventurers travel into the wilderness for days, or even weeks, at a time!

Some campers take in the wild seashore at Acadia National Park in Maine. Others enjoy rowing through the **pristine** waters of Minnesota's Boundary Waters Canoe Area Wilderness. Still others prefer to watch the brilliant sunsets in New Mexico's Carlsbad Caverns National Park. Most campsites offer many activities to choose from. Fishing, hiking, bicycling, and canoeing are popular ways to

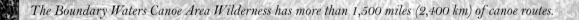

The Boundary Waters Canoe Area Wilderness has more than 1,500 miles (2,400 km) of canoe routes.

Spanning some 2,650 miles (4,260 km) along the West Coast, the Pacific Crest Trail runs from Mexico to Canada. On its way, the trail cuts through the scenic Cascade Mountains.

explore the wilderness. Campsites with more rugged **terrain** might offer rock climbing or horseback riding. Other sites are located near amusement parks.

However, many people camp to get away from their fast-paced lifestyles. Nature in its untouched beauty is stunning to observe. And, spending time in fresh air is energizing. Falling asleep to chirping crickets and waking up to singing birds can be a refreshing change.

NATURE BOUND

Since many activities are available to campers, it is important to choose the right location for your campout. Certain areas in national parks and state parks are set aside for camping. Yet, campers who want to make their own tracks stay in the backcountry. A permit is required for most places, including backcountry areas.

Many people travel to campgrounds by car. This is called car camping. Car campers usually stay at drive-in campsites. There, they can park their cars near their tents.

Drive-in sites are probably the most convenient places to camp. Motorcycles can easily access these sites, too. Certain sites have running water, electricity, and other **amenities**. Some drive-in campgrounds even have swimming pools and arcades!

Recreational vehicle (RV) campers need extra room for parking. RVs also require certain conveniences, such as electrical and water hookups. Special RV campgrounds provide these **accommodations**.

TIP *At certain times of the year, campgrounds fill up fast. If you are planning to camp during a holiday weekend, it is a good idea to reserve a spot well in advance.*

Backcountry campers sometimes travel to a site by canoe. They place all of their belongings inside the canoe in waterproof bags.

Many people prefer to camp in rugged areas with fewer comforts. They might stay in the backcountry, where motor vehicles are not allowed. Such areas must be reached on foot or horseback or by canoe or kayak (KEYE-ak). Traveling to these remote places can be a tempting challenge!

PACKING SMART

When packing, campers should plan for every situation and use the least possible amount of space and weight. This is especially important if they plan to carry everything in backpacks!

Certain items make camping more comfortable and enjoyable. Required equipment depends on the type of camping you plan to do. So, remember to think about your specific needs when choosing gear.

Car campers must pack a tent large enough to comfortably fit all the campers. Some people transport a canoe on the top of their car. Or, they might attach bicycles on the top or the back of their car. Most **RV**s have sleeping space and cooking stoves. So, RV campers do not need to bring a tent or a stove.

Campers who use kayaks, canoes, or motorcycles to reach their campsites pack light, small equipment. Hiking campers are particularly careful when packing their gear. They make sure to take only what they need. That is because they must carry their equipment in backpacks.

No matter which type of camping you choose, some items are essential. A trail map and a compass are useful tools for navigating. In addition, a lamp or a flashlight helps you get around in the dark.

A first aid kit is necessary in case of scrapes or bug bites. A basic kit should contain bandages, gauze, medical tape, small scissors, tweezers, soap, matches, disinfectant, calamine lotion, antibiotic cream, cotton swabs, and insect repellent.

First aid kit basics can help treat minor injuries.

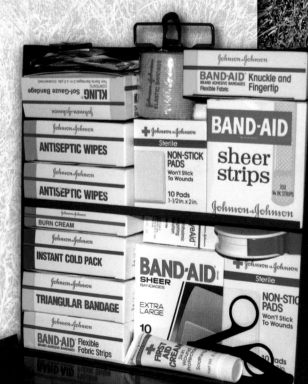

LAYER UP

Being prepared for anything includes being ready for all kinds of weather. In many areas, weather can change quickly. So, campers should dress in layers. By taking off or putting on layers, they can easily remain comfortable when conditions change.

Each layer should consist of a specific material. The layer closest to the body should be made of materials such as polyester or polypropylene. These fabrics remove moisture from the skin to prevent wetness.

On top of the first layer should be a layer that traps moisture from underneath and keeps the body warm. Wool or fleece fabrics are ideal. The outer layer should keep away wind, rain, and snow. Usually, a jacket or a pullover is best.

Many types of supplies protect campers from the elements. In wet weather, a raincoat and waterproof boots keep campers dry. On sunny days, wearing a good pair of sunglasses prevents eyestrain. To avoid sunburn, campers should always wear sunscreen with an **SPF** of at least 15.

Many campers bring hiking boots. To avoid painful blisters, break them in before your trip.

YOUR WILDERNESS WARDROBE

Packing for a variety of weather conditions can be a challenge. These tips will help you stay comfortable from head to toe.

- Wear a wide-brimmed hat to stay cool and to prevent a sunburned face and neck.

- Carry a bandanna. It is lightweight and can be used as a head covering, a sweatband, a bandage, or a sling.

- Bring a well-fitted pair of boots, especially if you plan to hike.

- Pack a pair of pants with lots of pockets, such as cargo pants. The pockets are useful for storing small items.

- On cool nights, wear a hat and a pair of fresh socks while sleeping. Otherwise, much of your body heat will escape.

- In heat and intense sun, wear light colors. Dark colors absorb more heat.

TENT CAMPING

Campers have several options for sleeping **accommodations**. **RV** campers usually sleep in their vehicles. Car, motorcycle, or hiking campers sleep in tents. There are many styles of tents to choose from. A-frame tents are triangle shaped. Tents can also be dome, **cylinder**, or umbrella shaped.

Early tents were made of **canvas**. Your grandparents probably camped in canvas tents! This material worked well for tents because it was **durable**. However, canvas tents were heavy, bulky, and hot. Today, tents are made of lighter materials, such as polyester or nylon. These materials breathe well and are more comfortable to sleep in.

Most modern tents have similar features. They have a rain fly, which covers the top of the tent. This layer protects the tent from rain soaking through. Most tents have a floor that is made of a strong, waterproof fabric. This material rises about six inches (15 cm) up the sides of the tent to prevent flooding during a storm.

The dome tent is the most popular type of tent for camping.
Its crisscrossing pole design helps it withstand heavy winds.

SLEEPING BAGS

After campers have chosen a good shelter, they must also select proper sleeping bags. Mummy bags and rectangular bags are the two basic choices.

Mummy bags are ideal for cold weather because they fit very snugly. They hold no extra space for air to sneak in, so they keep campers warm. Rectangular bags are best for warmer weather. These wider bags allow more room for air to flow.

There are several other things to consider when shopping for a sleeping bag. Bags have different types of

insulation. **Down**-filled bags are warm and long lasting, but they can be costly. **Synthetic**-filled bags do not last as long. However, they are more affordable and more resistant to wetness.

Remember to look at a bag's temperature rating, too. This number indicates the lowest temperature at which the bag will keep you warm. Finally, using a pad that fits under a sleeping bag also makes camping more comfortable!

A 40-degree-Fahrenheit (4°C) sleeping bag is ideal for warm weather. This bag will keep you comfortable as long as the outside temperature stays above 40°.

CHOOSING A SITE

After a good night's sleep, waking up to a beautiful view is thrilling! Most people look for a good view when selecting their campsite. But, campers must also keep safety in mind.

In case of heavy rain, campsites should be at least 200 feet (61 m) away from water sources. Tents should also be away from tall trees because branches could fall and hurt someone.

In the backcountry, there are no specific camping areas. Finding a campsite can be challenging. It is important for campers to impact nature as little as possible. So, they should set up camp in flat, open areas. That way, branches or rocks do not have to be moved. Remember, these natural surroundings are home to many creatures.

Once a site has been selected, it is time to set up camp! First, campers use a compass to position their tent. If they want the morning sun to enter the tent, a window should face east. After the tent is positioned, campers assemble it.

Set up your tent at least 15 feet (5 m) from the campfire area. In the backcountry, tents should be 200 feet (61 m) from trails and water sources.

TIP *Ask an adult to help you set up a tent in your backyard to practice camping. This will give you a preview of what camping is all about!*

Tents usually have step-by-step instructions for setup. First, campers unfold the material. After inserting the poles and driving the stakes into the ground, it is time to raise the tent. Make sure the stakes are pushed into the ground at an angle to secure the tent.

CAMP COOKING

After a long day of hiking or swimming, a good campfire meal is something to look forward to! It is easy to use twice the normal amount of daily energy while camping. So, campers should pack plenty of food and water for their trip.

Campers can bring any kind of food, as long as it is stored properly. Fresh food should be kept in a cooler. Many campers choose to bring **dehydrated** food because it is light and does not spoil quickly. Dehydrated meals are also easy to prepare. Just add water!

Clean water is a must. If there is no source of pure water at a campsite, campers bring their own water or **purification** system. They use a filter

Even if water found on the trail looks clean, it may contain harmful bacteria. Boiling the water over a campfire removes the bacteria.

or **purification** tablets to purify water. Or, they boil water for at least three minutes to make it drinkable.

Campers can cook foods over a campfire, a **portable** stove, or a grill. There are many kinds of portable stoves. Most often, they require fuels such as propane or white gas. The most common portable grills operate with

Campfire cooking is a lot of fun! But remember to always have an adult help you around the fire.

propane or charcoal. But, never use grills or stoves to heat a tent. These tools release a deadly gas, so they need proper **ventilation**.

CONSTRUCT A CAMPFIRE

Gathering around a crackling campfire to sing songs, tell stories, and roast marshmallows can be the highlight of a camping trip. If possible, campers should always use an existing fire pit. If there isn't one, just follow these steps to build your own campfire!

1. Find a spot at least 15 feet (5 m) away from tree trunks, thick plants, and your tent.

2. Build a mound of rocks or sand. This prevents heat from damaging soil.

3. Gather tinder, such as small dead twigs, dry bark, and leaves. Also find kindling. This includes larger dry sticks and fallen branches.

4. Place the tinder on top of the mound and surround it with the kindling.

5. Ask an adult to help you light the tinder on fire.

6. Add larger pieces of wood as the fire grows. Fires need oxygen, so leave some open space.

7. At the end of the night, slowly pour water over the fire to put it out. Make sure the fire is completely out, and never leave it unattended.

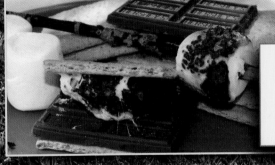

TASTY TREATS

No camper leaves home without marshmallows, graham crackers, and chocolate to make s'mores. But, here are two recipes for other great camping food!

BANANA BOATS

Ingredients for single serving:
- 1 banana
- peanut butter
- chocolate

Directions:

Slice banana from one long end to the other without cutting through the back side of the peel. Spread peanut butter in the middle of the banana and add chocolate. Adding marshmallows or caramel is also tasty! Wrap banana in foil and place on a grill. When ingredients are melted, your banana boat is ready to eat. It is easiest to eat with a spoon.

FOIL PACKS

Ingredients for single serving:
- 1/8–1/4 pound ground meat (optional)
- 1/2 potato, sliced
- 1/4 onion, sliced
- 1 medium carrot, sliced
- 1/4 green pepper, sliced

Directions:

Put ground meat on the center of a double layer of foil. Place carrot, potato, green pepper, and onion over meat. Fold foil to make a packet. With tongs, place foil pack on top of coals. Flip packet over when it sizzles. Flip often for about 7 to 10 minutes. Open carefully and enjoy!

WILDLIFE

Animals in the wild are exciting to observe. But, it is best to admire them from a distance. Most animals do not bother people unless they feel threatened. Still, wild creatures can be curious.

If animals smell something yummy, they might be tempted to search through a camper's gear to find food. Bears and raccoons are commonly known to do this. Campers should never feed wild animals because it interferes with their natural eating habits. This encourages

You can learn a lot about an animal's way of life just by observing it!

Campers hang food at least 15 feet (5 m) from the ground and far out on a limb.

them to rely on obtaining human food. Animals can become **aggressive** to get human food.

There are several ways for campers to protect their supplies. They can lock their food inside a vehicle or in a metal box. Or, they can use a rope to hang food from a high tree branch so animals cannot reach it. Some people also attach an upside-down can to the rope a few feet above the food. This prevents squirrels from climbing down the rope and into the gear.

STAY SAFE

For some people, the joy of camping is finding their way in the wilderness. But, campers should never wander off by themselves. And, they should always tell an adult their plans. Many campgrounds offer maps of trails. Some sites have park rangers who can help lost campers, too.

However, backcountry campers must be able to navigate on their own. In addition to maps, some of them use a compass or a Global Positioning System (GPS) receiver. GPS uses **satellites** that transmit signals to determine a person's location. It is **accurate** within 50 feet (15 m)!

However, certain situations may arise that campers cannot expect. Common problems are skin irritations from poisonous plants, as well as painful or itchy bug bites. A first aid kit is helpful for these situations. And if you spend time in thick forests, be sure to occasionally check yourself for ticks.

Campers should also remember to drink lots of water. Sweating and being in the sun cause the body to lose more

water than usual. **Dehydration** happens if the body has not received enough liquids. It can have serious effects.

Backcountry campers should carry a topographic map. This type of map offers detailed pictures of terrain, such as cliffs, mountains, and ridges.

COURTEOUS CAMPING

Most campers enjoy the same outdoor camping activities that you do. And, many of them like to meet others who share their interests. So, talking with people and making new friends is always welcome. Just make sure your group knows where you are!

Some people go camping to escape from crowds of people and activity. Running around, making loud noises, or blasting a stereo might ruin their vacation. Be especially mindful of this at night, when people are resting.

In addition to respecting others, it is important to respect the **environment**. Campers observe a rule called "pack it in, pack it out." This means they should make minimal impact on wildlife. Campers pack their garbage in small plastic bags and make sure it leaves with them.

Many campgrounds have toilet facilities. But, backcountry campers do not have this luxury. Instead, they dig a hole in the ground to use as a "toilet." The hole must be at least 200 feet (61 m) from water and far from trails. After using it, campers cover it with natural materials, such as leaves.

Camping is a wonderful opportunity to learn about our natural world. Just like Joe and his grandpa discovered, nature often leaves us with a feeling of wonder and amazement!

Camping is a great way to spend time with friends and family. You might make some new friends, too!

GLOSSARY

accommodation - something supplied for convenience or to satisfy a need. Accommodations can include lodging, food, or other services.

accurate - free of errors.

aggressive - displaying hostility.

amenity - something that brings comfort, convenience, or enjoyment.

canvas - a firm, closely woven cloth usually made of linen, hemp, or cotton. It is used to make clothing, tents, and sails.

cylinder - a solid figure of two parallel circles bound by a curved surface. A soda can is an example of a cylinder.

dehydration - the result of too little water. When used or lost fluid is not replaced, a person becomes dehydrated. To dehydrate a food, the water is removed from it.

down - soft, fluffy feathers.

durable - able to exist for a long time without weakening.

environment - all the surroundings that affect the growth and well-being of a living thing.

insulation - material used to keep something from losing or transferring electricity, heat, or sound.

portable - able to be carried or moved.

pristine - not spoiled, corrupted, or polluted.

purify - to make or become pure.

recreational vehicle (RV) - a vehicle designed for recreational use, such as camping.

satellite - a manufactured object that orbits Earth.

SPF - sun protection factor. A classification of the U.S. Food and Drug Administration of the degree to which a sunblock or a sunscreen will protect the skin from sunburn.

stance - a way of standing or being placed.

synthetic - substances or products made by chemical synthesis. These include plastics and artificial fibers.

terrain - the physical features of an area of land. Mountains, rivers, and canyons can all be part of a terrain.

ventilation - circulation of air.

WEB SITES

To learn more about camping, visit ABDO Publishing Company on the World Wide Web at **www.abdopublishing.com**. Web sites about camping are featured on our Book Links page. These links are routinely monitored and updated to provide the most current information available.

INDEX